THREE
Moments
A DAY

galison

THREE
Moments
A DAY

galison

www.galison.com f 🎨 @galisongift

70 West 36th Street, 11th Floor

New York, NY 10018

Interior design by Katie Jennings Campbell

Images used under license from Shutterstock.com

ISBN: 978-0-7353-5504-0

ISBN: 978-0-9982297-6-8 (Sterling)

First Edition: January 2018

Designed and printed in the United States of America.

10 9 8 7 6 5 4 3 2 1

What you focus on EXPANDS.

Every day of our lives is not a 24/7 party. We face challenges, heartbreaks, even devastation. But we also experience amazing moments of joy right in the midst of it all. That phone call or outreached hand that comes just when you need it. A sloppy, no-holds-barred kiss from a toddler or a dog. A sunset unlike any other you've ever seen before. The feel of your favorite blanket warm and comforting from the dryer. The sudden realization that a difficult time brought about a blessing in disguise.

Three Moments a Day is designed to help you appreciate these moments that reflect the beauty in our imperfect lives, so you can get through all the other times that feel covered in mud (or even quicksand!). Spend some time jotting down your three best moments of joy every night before going to bed, and your eyes will be opened to all that your life has to offer. (You might even have trouble narrowing your moments down to just three!)

Focus on the good—the gifts we are given each day—and you'll know the secret to living a full life.

THE MOMENTS
OF HAPPINESS
WE ENJOY
TAKE US
BY SURPRISE.
IT IS NOT
THAT WE
SEIZE THEM,
BUT THAT
THEY
SEIZE US.

—Ashley Montagu

My three moments of joy today:

1. _____

_____

2. _____

_____

3. _____

_____

There are souls in this
world which have
THE GIFT OF
FINDING JOY
EVERYWHERE
and of leaving it behind
them when they go.

—Jean Paul

My three moments of joy today:

1. _____

_____

2. _____

_____

3. _____

_____

There is a
calmness to a life
lived in gratitude,
A QUIET JOY.

—Ralph H. Blum

My three moments of joy today:

1. _____

_____

2. _____

_____

3. _____

_____

JOY COMES IN SIPS, NOT GULPS.

—Sharon Draper

My three moments of joy today:

1. _____

   _____

2. _____

   _____

3. _____

   _____

It is during our darkest
moments that we must
FOCUS TO SEE
THE LIGHT.

—Aristotle

My three moments of joy today:

1. _____

_____

2. _____

_____

3. _____

_____

WE DO NOT REMEMBER DAYS; *we remember moments.*

—Cesare Pavese

Today's Date ....

My three moments of joy today:

1. _____

   _____

2. _____

   _____

3. _____

   _____

LOOK AT
EVERYTHING
AS THOUGH YOU
WERE SEEING
IT EITHER FOR
THE FIRST OR
LAST TIME.

—Betty Smith

My three moments of joy today:

1. _____

_____

2. _____

_____

3. _____

_____

I don't have to chase extraordinary moments to find happiness—

IT'S RIGHT IN FRONT OF ME IF I'M PAYING ATTENTION.

—Brené Brown

My three moments of joy today:

1. _____

_____

2. _____

_____

3. _____

_____

SLOW DOWN
AND ENJOY LIFE.

It's not only the scenery you miss by going too fast—

YOU ALSO MISS THE SENSE OF WHERE YOU ARE GOING AND WHY.

—Eddie Cantor

My three moments of joy today:

1. _____

_____

2. _____

_____

3. _____

_____

LIFE ISN'T A MATTER OF MILESTONES,

but of moments.

—Rose Kennedy

My three moments of joy today:

1. _____

_____

2. _____

_____

3. _____

_____

We can choose to FOCUS ON THE BEAUTY of the now.

—Steve Gleason

My three moments of joy today:

1. _____

_____

2. _____

_____

3. _____

_____

THERE ARE
MOMENTS
WHEN ALL
ANXIETY AND
STATED TOIL
ARE BECALMED
IN THE INFINITE
LEISURE AND
REPOSE OF NATURE.

—Henry David Thoreau

My three moments of joy today:

1. _____

_____

2. _____

_____

3. _____

_____

THE SUN DOES NOT
SHINE FOR A FEW
TREES AND FLOWERS,
but for the wide
worlds joy.

—Henry Ward Beecher

My three moments of joy today:

1. _____

_____

2. _____

_____

3. _____

_____

One doesn't recognize THE REALLY IMPORTANT MOMENTS IN ONE'S LIFE until it's too late.

—Agatha Christie

My three moments of joy today:

1. _____
_____

2. _____
_____

3. _____
_____

Find joy

IN EVERYTHING YOU CHOOSE TO DO.

—Chuck Palahniuk

My three moments of joy today:

1. _____

   _____

2. _____

   _____

3. _____

   _____

SO OFTEN, WE
DON'T REALIZE
THAT THE VERY
MOMENTS IN WHICH
WE LIVE BECOME
OUR HISTORY,
OUR STORY.

—Deborah Wiles

My three moments of joy today:

1. _____

_____

2. _____

_____

3. _____

_____

A TABLE,
a chair,
A BOWL OF FRUIT
and a violin;
WHAT ELSE DOES
A MAN NEED
TO BE HAPPY?

—Albert Einstein

My three moments of joy today:

1. _____

_____

2. _____

_____

3. _____

_____

You're only here

FOR A
MATTER OF
MOMENTS.

—Tim Conway

My three moments of joy today:

1. _____

_____

2. _____

_____

3. _____

_____

WE CANNOT
CURE THE WORLD
OF SORROWS,
but we can choose
to live in joy.

—Joseph Campbell

My three moments of joy today:

1. _____

    _____

2. _____

    _____

3. _____

    _____

WHAT IS
INTERESTING IN
LIFE IS ALL THE
CRACKS AND
ALL THE FLAWS
AND ALL THE
MOMENTS THAT
ARE NOT PERFECT.

—Clémence Poésy

My three moments of joy today:

1. _____

   _____

2. _____

   _____

3. _____

   _____

LIFE IS A WAVE,

which in no two consecutive moments of its existence is composed of the same particles.

—John Tyndall

Today's Date ....

My three moments of joy today:

1. _____

   _____

2. _____

   _____

3. _____

   _____

WE CAN ONLY BE
SAID TO BE ALIVE
in those moments
when our hearts
are conscious of
our treasures.

—Thornton Wilder

My three moments of joy today:

1. _____

_____

2. _____

_____

3. _____

_____

YOU CAN SEE
AND YOU
CAN LISTEN,
BUT YOU HAVE
TO HAVE THOSE
MOMENTS
IN WHICH
YOU FEEL.

—Mike Krzyzewski

My three moments of joy today:

1. _____

   _____

2. _____

   _____

3. _____

   _____

HOLD ON TO THOSE MOMENTS

when a little spark

cuts through the fog

AND NUDGES YOU.

—Rufus Wainwright

Today's Date _____

My three moments of joy today:

1. _____

   _____

2. _____

   _____

3. _____

   _____

FIND THE
stolen
moments
OF JOY IN
ALL YOU DO.

—Niecy Nash

Today's Date _____

My three moments of joy today:

1. _____

_____

2. _____

_____

3. _____

_____

IF YOU
SURRENDER
COMPLETELY
TO THE
MOMENTS AS
THEY PASS,
YOU LIVE MORE
RICHLY THOSE
MOMENTS.

—Anne Morrow Lindbergh

My three moments of joy today:

1. _____

_____

2. _____

_____

3. _____

_____

Happiness is
not having
what you want.

IT IS

APPRECIATING

what you have.

—Anonymous

My three moments of joy today:

1. _____

_____

2. _____

_____

3. _____

_____

Little moments
CAN HAVE
A FEELING
and a texture
THAT IS
VERY REAL.

—Ralph Fiennes

My three moments of joy today:

1. _____

   _____

2. _____

   _____

3. _____

   _____

THE MOMENTS WHEN YOU HAVE TRULY LIVED ARE THE MOMENTS WHEN YOU HAVE DONE THINGS IN THE SPIRIT OF LOVE.

—Henry Drummond

My three moments of joy today:

1. _____

_____

2. _____

_____

3. _____

_____

PAY ATTENTION

to the moments

when you've felt

on top of the world.

—Sebastian Stan

My three moments of joy today:

1. _____

_____

2. _____

_____

3. _____

_____

PERFECT HAPPINESS

is a beautiful sunset,
THE GIGGLE OF
A GRANDCHILD,
the first snowfall.

—Sharon Draper

My three moments of joy today:

1. _____

   _____

2. _____

   _____

3. _____

   _____

THERE ARE PLACES
AND MOMENTS IN
WHICH ONE IS SO
COMPLETELY ALONE
THAT ONE SEES
THE WORLD
ENTIRE.

—Jules Renard

My three moments of joy today:

1. _____

   _____

2. _____

   _____

3. _____

   _____

The most pivotal moments in people's lives

REVOLVE AROUND EMOTIONS.

—Brandon Stanton

My three moments of joy today:

1. _____

_____

2. _____

_____

3. _____

_____

Stories are
THE RICH,
UNSEEN
UNDERLAYER
of the
MOST ORDINARY
MOMENTS.

—*Mary Gaitskill*

My three moments of joy today:

1. _____

_____

2. _____

_____

3. _____

_____

JOY
IS NOT
IN THINGS;

IT IS IN
US.

—Richard Wagner

My three moments of joy today:

1. _____

   _____

2. _____

   _____

3. _____

   _____

There are
moments when,
whatever the posture
of the body,
THE SOUL IS
ON ITS KNEES.

—Victor Hugo

My three moments of joy today:

1. _____

_____

2. _____

_____

3. _____

_____

THE REASON PEOPLE
FIND IT SO HARD TO
BE HAPPY IS THAT
THEY ALWAYS SEE
the past
BETTER THAN IT WAS,
the present
WORSE THAN IT IS,
and the future
LESS RESOLVED THAN
IT WILL BE.

—Marcel Pagnol

My three moments of joy today:

1. _____

_____

2. _____

_____

3. _____

_____

IT WAS
JUST ONE
OF THOSE
MOMENTS IN
THE UNIVERSE
THAT WAS
MINE.

—Carlton Fisk

My three moments of joy today:

1. _____

_____

2. _____

_____

3. _____

_____

Those who wish
TO SING
will always find
A SONG.

—Swedish proverb

My three moments of joy today:

1. _____

_____

2. _____

_____

3. _____

_____

PLAY THE
MOMENTS,
pause the memories,
STOP THE PAIN,
*and rewind
the happiness.*

—Anonymous

My three moments of joy today:

1. _____

   _____

2. _____

   _____

3. _____

   _____

JOY IS THE
HOLY FIRE
THAT KEEPS
OUR PURPOSE
WARM
AND OUR
INTELLIGENCE
AGLOW.

—Helen Keller

My three moments of joy today:

1. _____

_____

2. _____

_____

3. _____

_____

This moment

CONTAINS
ALL
MOMENTS.

—C. S. Lewis

My three moments of joy today:

1. _____

   _____

2. _____

   _____

3. _____

   _____

Folks are usually about as HAPPY as they make their minds up to be.

—attributed to Abraham Lincoln

My three moments of joy today:

1. _____

_____

2. _____

_____

3. _____

_____

NO MATTER
HOW HARD
TIMES GET,
THERE ARE
ALWAYS THOSE
MIRACLE
MOMENTS
THAT LIFT YOU
BACK ON YOUR
FEET.

—Anonymous

My three moments of joy today:

1. _____

   _____

2. _____

   _____

3. _____

   _____

If you carry
JOY IN
YOUR
HEART,
you can heal
any moment.

—Carlos Santana

My three moments of joy today:

1. _____

_____

2. _____

_____

3. _____

_____

THINK JOY,
talk joy,
PRACTICE JOY,
share joy,
SATURATE
YOUR MIND
WITH JOY...

—Norman Vincent Peale

My three moments of joy today:

1. _____

_____

2. _____

_____

3. _____

_____

Who will tell whether one

happy moment of love,

or the joy of breathing

or walking on a bright morning

and smelling the fresh air,

is not worth all the suffering

and effort which life implies?

—*Erich Fromm*

My three moments of joy today:

1. _____

   _____

2. _____

   _____

3. _____

   _____

COUNT YOUR LIFE WITH SMILES— NOT TEARS.

—Dixie Willson

My three moments of joy today:

1. _____

_____

2. _____

_____

3. _____

_____

The happiness
of your life
DEPENDS UPON
THE QUALITY OF
YOUR THOUGHTS.

—Marcus Aurelius

My three moments of joy today:

1. _____

_____

2. _____

_____

3. _____

_____

LIFE IS
A JOURNEY,
and if you fall in love with the journey,
YOU WILL BE IN
LOVE FOREVER.

—Peter Hagerty

My three moments of joy today:

1. _____

_____

2. _____

_____

3. _____

_____

IT ISN'T WHAT
YOU HAVE,
OR WHO YOU ARE,
OR WHERE
YOU ARE,
OR WHAT YOU
ARE DOING
THAT MAKES YOU
HAPPY OR UNHAPPY.
IT IS WHAT YOU
THINK ABOUT.

—Dale Carnegie

My three moments of joy today:

1. _____

_____

2. _____

_____

3. _____

_____

IT'S A HELLUVA START,

being able to recognize
what makes you happy.

—Lucille Ball

My three moments of joy today:

1. _____

_____

2. _____

_____

3. _____

_____

When one door
of happiness closes,
another opens,
BUT OFTEN WE LOOK
SO LONG AT THE
CLOSED DOOR THAT
WE DO NOT SEE THE
ONE THAT HAS BEEN
OPENED FOR US.

—Helen Keller

My three moments of joy today:

1. _____

_____

2. _____

_____

3. _____

_____

EVERYONE'S LIFE HAS THESE MOMENTS, WHERE ONE THING LEADS TO ANOTHER.

—Peter Jackson

My three moments of joy today:

1. _____

_____

2. _____

_____

3. _____

_____

It is more fitting
for a man to
LAUGH
AT LIFE
than to lament
over it.

—Seneca

My three moments of joy today:

1. _____

_____

2. _____

_____

3. _____

_____

*Life is
really simple,*

BUT WE INSIST

ON MAKING IT

COMPLICATED.

—Confucius

My three moments of joy today:

1. _____

_____

2. _____

_____

3. _____

_____

I REMEMBER
THE STORY OF
THE OLD MAN
WHO SAID ON HIS
DEATHBED THAT
HE HAD HAD
A LOT OF TROUBLE
IN HIS LIFE,
MOST OF WHICH HAD
NEVER HAPPENED.

—Winston Churchill

My three moments of joy today:

1. _____

    _____

2. _____

    _____

3. _____

    _____

The foolish man seeks happiness in the distance. THE WISE GROWS IT UNDER HIS FEET.

—James Oppenheim

My three moments of joy today:

1. _____

_____

2. _____

_____

3. _____

_____

HAPPINESS IS NOT THE ABSENCE OF PROBLEMS,

but the ability to deal with them.

— Charles de Montesquieu

My three moments of joy today:

1. _____

_____

2. _____

_____

3. _____

_____

NO MAN IS HAPPY WHO DOES NOT THINK HIMSELF SO.

—Publilius Syrus

My three moments of joy today:

1. _____

   _____

2. _____

   _____

3. _____

   _____

The greater part of
our happiness or misery

DEPENDS
UPON OUR
DISPOSITIONS,

and not upon

our circumstances.

—*Martha Washington*

My three moments of joy today:

1. _____

   _____

2. _____

   _____

3. _____

   _____

*Just because it
didn't last forever*

DOESN'T MEAN
IT WASN'T
WORTH YOUR
WHILE.

—Anonymous

My three moments of joy today:

1. _____

_____

2. _____

_____

3. _____

_____

HAPPINESS
ALWAYS LOOKS SMALL
WHILE YOU HOLD IT
IN YOUR HANDS,
BUT LET IT GO,
AND YOU LEARN
AT ONCE HOW BIG
AND PRECIOUS IT IS.

—Maxim Gorky

My three moments of joy today:

1. _____

_____

2. _____

_____

3. _____

_____

IN OUR DARKEST MOMENTS,

you have to find the humor, and you have to find the lightness.

—Corey Hawkins

My three moments of joy today:

1. _____
   _____

2. _____
   _____

3. _____
   _____

Plenty of people miss
their share of happiness,
NOT BECAUSE THEY
NEVER FOUND IT,
but because they
didn't stop to enjoy it.

—William Feather

My three moments of joy today:

1. _____

_____

2. _____

_____

3. _____

_____

IF YOU ARE TOO BUSY TO LAUGH,

YOU ARE TOO BUSY.

—*Anonymous*

My three moments of joy today:

1. _____

_____

2. _____

_____

3. _____

_____

We don't always choose moments...

SOMETIMES

THEY

CHOOSE US.

—Loretta Lynch

My three moments of joy today:

1. _____

_____

2. _____

_____

3. _____

_____

IF...HAPPINESS
DEPENDS ON
a good breakfast,
FLOWERS IN
THE YARD,
a drink or
A NAP,
then we are more
likely to live with quite
a bit of happiness.

—Andy Rooney

My three moments of joy today:

1. _____

_____

2. _____

_____

3. _____

_____

SOME OF THE
FUNNIEST,
MOST BEAUTIFUL,
AND TOUCHING
MOMENTS

HAPPEN WHEN
YOU LEAST
EXPECT IT.

—Bryce Dallas Howard

My three moments of joy today:

1. _____

_____

2. _____

_____

3. _____

_____

ENJOY
YOUR OWN LIFE
without comparing it
with that of another.

—Marquis de Condorcet

My three moments of joy today:

1. _____

   _____

2. _____

   _____

3. _____

   _____

I AM
SENSIBLE
of the
VELOCITY
of the
MOMENTS...

—*Harold Brodkey*

My three moments of joy today:

1. _____

_____

2. _____

_____

3. _____

_____

OPTIMISM IS
A HAPPINESS
MAGNET.
IF YOU
STAY POSITIVE,
GOOD THINGS
AND GOOD
PEOPLE WILL
BE DRAWN
TO YOU.

—Mary Lou Retton

My three moments of joy today:

1. _____

_____

2. _____

_____

3. _____

_____

In the
quiet moments,
THE
DISCOVERIES
ARE MADE.

—Vera Farmiga

My three moments of joy today:

1. _____

   _____

2. _____

   _____

3. _____

   _____

BEING HAPPY
DOESN'T MEAN
EVERYTHING
IS PERFECT.

It means you've decided to look beyond the imperfections.

—Anonymous

My three moments of joy today:

1. _____

_____

2. _____

_____

3. _____

_____

I AM
WORKING
ON FINDING
PEACE & JOY
IN THE
MOMENTS
WE HAVE
BEEN GIVEN.

—Taya Kyle

My three moments of joy today:

1. _____

_____

2. _____

_____

3. _____

_____

If you spend your whole life waiting for the storm,

YOU'LL NEVER ENJOY THE SUNSHINE.

—Morris West

My three moments of joy today:

1. _____

   _____

2. _____

   _____

3. _____

   _____

SHOW UP STRONG FOR THE MOMENTS THAT REALLY MATTER

with family, friends, and community.

—Andie MacDowell

Today's Date ....

My three moments of joy today:

1. _____

_____

2. _____

_____

3. _____

_____

LIFE WILL
BRING YOU
PAIN ALL
BY ITSELF.
YOUR
RESPONSIBILITY
IS TO
CREATE JOY.

—Milton Erickson

My three moments of joy today:

1. _____

   _____

2. _____

   _____

3. _____

   _____

Even in our
darkest moments
we try and find

SOMETHING

BEAUTIFUL.

—Eddie Vedder

Today's Date _____

My three moments of joy today:

1. _____

   _____

2. _____

   _____

3. _____

   _____

FIND A PLACE
INSIDE WHERE
THERE'S JOY,
and the joy will
burn out the pain.

—Joseph Campbell

My three moments of joy today:

1. _____

_____

2. _____

_____

3. _____

_____

THE BEST MOMENTS CAN'T BE PRECONCEIVED.

—*Brad Pitt*

Today's Date ....

My three moments of joy today:

1. _____

   _____

2. _____

   _____

3. _____

   _____

Each day
HOLDS A
SURPRISE.

—Henri Nouwen

Today's Date _____

My three moments of joy today:

1. _____

   _____

2. _____

   _____

3. _____

   _____

Moments like this
come and go
UNLESS WE
SEIZE THEM AT
THEIR HEIGHT.

—Jonathan Kozol

My three moments of joy today:

1. _____

   _____

2. _____

   _____

3. _____

   _____

JOY IS A NET OF LOVE BY WHICH YOU CAN CATCH SOULS.

—Mother Teresa

My three moments of joy today:

1. _____

_____

2. _____

_____

3. _____

_____

You get these
moments in the ring
THAT LAST
FOREVER.

—Sugar Ray Leonard

My three moments of joy today:

1. _____

   _____

2. _____

   _____

3. _____

   _____

If the simple things of nature have a message that you understand, REJOICE, FOR YOUR SOUL IS ALIVE.

—Eleonora Duse

My three moments of joy today:

1. _____

   _____

2. _____

   _____

3. _____

   _____

JOY IS WHAT
HAPPENS
WHEN WE
ALLOW
OURSELVES TO
RECOGNIZE
HOW GOOD
THINGS
REALLY ARE.

—Marianne Williamson

Today's Date ....

My three moments of joy today:

1. _____

   _____

2. _____

   _____

3. _____

   _____

Find what you
love to do,
FIND THE
JOY IN IT,
and express yourself
through your passion.

—Barry Williams

My three moments of joy today:

1. _____

_____

2. _____

_____

3. _____

_____

We all find joy
and radiance
AND A REASON
TO MOVE ON
even in the

most dire of
circumstances.

—Ishmael Beah

Today's Date ....

My three moments of joy today:

1. _____

   _____

2. _____

   _____

3. _____

   _____

STOP
AND TAKE IN
THE BEAUTY
OF AN
ORDINARY DAY.

—Jennifer Garner

My three moments of joy today:

1. _____

_____

2. _____

_____

3. _____

_____

Man cannot live without JOY.

—Thomas Aquinas

My three moments of joy today:

1. _____

   _____

2. _____

   _____

3. _____

   _____

I LOVE THIS LIFE.

I feel like I am always catching my breath and saying,

'OH! WILL YOU LOOK AT THAT?'

—Harold Feinstein

My three moments of joy today:

1. _____

   _____

2. _____

   _____

3. _____

   _____

WE SHOULD
ALL DO WHAT,
IN THE LONG RUN,
GIVES US JOY,
EVEN IF IT IS
ONLY PICKING
GRAPES OR
SORTING THE
LAUNDRY.

—E. B. White

My three moments of joy today:

1. _____

_____

2. _____

_____

3. _____

_____

It is a fine
seasoning for joy to
THINK OF
THOSE
WE LOVE.

—Moliere

My three moments of joy today:

1. _____

_____

2. _____

_____

3. _____

_____

JOY COMES
FROM PLACES
YOU LEAST
EXPECT IT.
It's usually the
simple things.

—Dave Gahan

My three moments of joy today:

1. _____

_____

2. _____

_____

3. _____

_____

I'M TRYING
TO FIND A
LITTLE JOY
AND HAPPINESS,
A LOT OF
GIGGLES–
AND MAYBE
SOME PRETTY
SHOES.

—Tracee Ellis Ross

My three moments of joy today:

1. _____

   _____

2. _____

   _____

3. _____

   _____

A DOSE OF JOY

is a

spiritual cure.

—Ed Sullivan

FOR YOU

My three moments of joy today:

1. _____

_____

2. _____

_____

3. _____

_____

*I am happier
when I love*
THAN WHEN
I AM LOVED.

—Isabel Allende

My three moments of joy today:

1. _____

_____

2. _____

_____

3. _____

_____

IT IS THE
EXPERIENCES,
THE MEMORIES,
THE GREAT
TRIUMPHANT JOY
OF LIVING TO THE
FULLEST EXTENT
IN WHICH
REAL MEANING
IS FOUND.

—Christopher McCandless

My three moments of joy today:

1. _____

_____

2. _____

_____

3. _____

_____

It's always such a joy
that you wake up
in the morning
AND THERE'S
WORK TO DO.

—Jerome Lawrence

My three moments of joy today:

1. _____

_____

2. _____

_____

3. _____

_____

If you emanate joy,

IT COMES
BACK TO YOU.

—Robin Wright

My three moments of joy today:

1. _____

_____

2. _____

_____

3. _____

_____

GENUINE
HAPPINESS
COMES FROM
WITHIN,
AND OFTEN IT
COMES IN
SPONTANEOUS
FEELINGS
OF JOY.

—Andrew Weil

My three moments of joy today:

1. _____

_____

2. _____

_____

3. _____

_____

A PROPENSITY
TO HOPE AND JOY
IS REAL RICHES;

one to fear and

sorrow, real poverty.

—David Hume

My three moments of joy today:

1. _____

   _____

2. _____

   _____

3. _____

   _____

FIND
joy and solace
IN THE
SIMPLE.

—Wayne Dyer

Today's Date ....

My three moments of joy today:

1. _____

_____

2. _____

_____

3. _____

_____

THE JOY OF THE MIND IS THE MEASURE OF ITS STRENGTH.

—Ninon de l'Enclos

My three moments of joy today:

1. _____

_____

2. _____

_____

3. _____

_____

JOY

is not the negation
of pain, but rather
acknowledging the
presence of pain
and feeling happiness
in spite of it.

—Lupita Nyong'o

My three moments of joy today:

1. _____

   _____

2. _____

   _____

3. _____

   _____

HOPE
IS A STATE
OF THE MIND,

not of the world.

—Václav Havel

My three moments of joy today:

1. _____

_____

2. _____

_____

3. _____

_____

TO MAKE OTHERS
LESS HAPPY
IS A CRIME.
TO MAKE
OURSELVES
UNHAPPY IS
WHERE ALL
CRIME STARTS.
WE MUST TRY TO
CONTRIBUTE JOY
TO THE WORLD.

—Roger Ebert

My three moments of joy today:

1. _____

   _____

2. _____

   _____

3. _____

   _____

JOY IS THE WILL
WHICH LABOURS,
which overcomes
obstacles,
WHICH KNOWS
TRIUMPH.

—William Butler Yeats

My three moments of joy today:

1. _____

_____

2. _____

_____

3. _____

_____

Side by side
with grief
LIES JOY.

—Fran Drescher

My three moments of joy today:

1. _____

_____

2. _____

_____

3. _____

_____

THE SECRET TO LIFE

IS FINDING JOY IN ORDINARY THINGS.

—Ruth Reichl

My three moments of joy today:

1. _____

_____

2. _____

_____

3. _____

_____

I choose to
spend my life
CRAFTING
A JOY.

—Jason Mraz

My three moments of joy today:

1. _____

_____

2. _____

_____

3. _____

_____

Everywhere across whatever sorrows of which our life is woven, SOME RADIANT JOY WILL GAILY FLASH PAST.

—Nikolai Gogol

My three moments of joy today:

1. _____

   _____

2. _____

   _____

3. _____

   _____

CONQUERING ANY DIFFICULTY ALWAYS GIVES ONE A SECRET JOY.

—Henri-Frédéric Amiel

My three moments of joy today:

1. _____

_____

2. _____

_____

3. _____

_____

I believe
ENLIGHTENMENT
or
REVELATION
comes in daily life.

I look for joy,
the peace of action.

—Paulo Coelho

My three moments of joy today:

1. _____

_____

2. _____

_____

3. _____

_____

MAKE SPACE IN YOUR LIFE FOR THE THINGS THAT MATTER, FOR

family and friends,

love and generosity,

fun and joy.

—Jonathan Sacks

My three moments of joy today:

1. _____

   _____

2. _____

   _____

3. _____

   _____

LIFE

IS MADE UP

OF SMALL

PLEASURES.

—Norman Lear

My three moments of joy today:

1. _____

   _____

2. _____

   _____

3. _____

   _____

Do not be afraid
that joy will
make the pain worse;
IT IS NEEDED
like the air we breathe.

—Göran Persson

My three moments of joy today:

1. _____

_____

2. _____

_____

3. _____

_____

I happy am,

JOY

is my name.

—William Blake

My three moments of joy today:

1. _____

_____

2. _____

_____

3. _____

_____

A LAUGH, TO BE JOYOUS, MUST FLOW FROM A JOYOUS HEART, FOR WITHOUT KINDNESS, THERE CAN BE NO TRUE JOY.

—Thomas Carlyle

My three moments of joy today:

1. _____

   _____

2. _____

   _____

3. _____

   _____

It's a mistake
to miss out on
JOY
just because you
have pain.

—Taya Kyle

Today's Date ....

My three moments of joy today:

1. _____

_____

2. _____

_____

3. _____

_____

There is no
such thing as
THE PURSUIT
OF HAPPINESS,
but there is
THE DISCOVERY
OF JOY.

—Joyce Grenfell

My three moments of joy today:

1. _____

_____

2. _____

_____

3. _____

_____

JOY COMES, GRIEF GOES, WE KNOW NOT HOW.

—James Russell Lowell

Today's Date ....

My three moments of joy today:

1. _____

   _____

2. _____

   _____

3. _____

   _____

I want to know
WHERE
JOY
LIVES.

—Goldie Hawn

My three moments of joy today:

1. _____

   _____

2. _____

   _____

3. _____

   _____

One should
sympathise with

THE COLOUR,

THE BEAUTY,

THE JOY OF LIFE.

—Oscar Wilde

My three moments of joy today:

1. _____

_____

2. _____

_____

3. _____

_____

YOUR JOY
COMES FROM
HOW YOU
THINK,
THE CHOICES
THAT WE
MAKE IN LIFE.

—Joyce Meyer

My three moments of joy today:

1. _____

_____

2. _____

_____

3. _____

_____

When joy is a
HABIT,
love is a
REFLEX.

—Bob Goff

My three moments of joy today:

1. _____

_____

2. _____

_____

3. _____

_____

We are all dreaming of some magical rose garden over the horizon— INSTEAD OF ENJOYING THE ROSES THAT ARE BLOOMING OUTSIDE OUR WINDOWS TODAY.

—Dale Carnegie

My three moments of joy today:

1. _____

   _____

2. _____

   _____

3. _____

   _____

FOR IN THE
DEW OF
LITTLE THINGS
THE HEART
FINDS ITS
MORNING AND
IS REFRESHED.

—Khalil Gibran

My three moments of joy today:

1. _____

_____

2. _____

_____

3. _____

_____

IF MY WORLD
WERE TO CAVE
IN TOMORROW,
I'd look back on
all the pleasures,
excitement, and
worthwhileness
I have been lucky
enough to have had.

—Audrey Hepburn

My three moments of joy today:

1. _____

_____

2. _____

_____

3. _____

_____

The present moment
is filled with
JOY AND
HAPPINESS.
If you are attentive,
you will see it.

—Thich Nhat Hanh